*f*RESH *f*OODS

Mini Vegetable Quiches

2 cups cut-up vegetables (bell peppers, broccoli, zucchini and/or
  carrots)
2 tablespoons chopped green onion
2 tablespoons **FLEISCHMANN'S®** Original Margarine
4 (8-inch) flour tortillas, each cut into 8 triangles
1 cup **EGG BEATERS®** Healthy Real Egg Product
1 cup fat-free (skim) milk
½ teaspoon dried basil leaves

In medium nonstick skillet, over medium-high heat, sauté vegetables and green onion in margarine until tender.

Arrange 4 tortilla triangles in each of 8 (6-ounce) greased custard cups or ramekins, placing points of tortilla triangles at center of bottom of each cup and pressing lightly to form shape of cup. Divide vegetable mixture evenly among cups. In small bowl, combine Egg Beaters®, milk and basil. Pour evenly over vegetable mixture. Place cups on baking sheet. Bake at 375°F for 20 to 25 minutes or until puffed and knife inserted into centers comes out clean. Let stand 5 minutes before serving.   *Makes 8 servings*

Fresh foods

Puff Pancake with Summer Berries

Summer Berries (recipe follows)
4 tablespoons butter or margarine, divided
2 eggs
½ cup all-purpose flour
½ cup milk
1 tablespoon sugar
¼ teaspoon salt

1. Prepare Summer Berries; set aside. Preheat oven to 425°F. Place 2 tablespoons butter in ovenproof skillet. Place skillet in oven 3 minutes or until butter is bubbly. Swirl pan to coat bottom and side.

2. Beat eggs in medium bowl with electric mixer at high speed. Add flour, milk, remaining 2 tablespoons butter, sugar and salt; beat until smooth.

3. Pour batter into prepared skillet. Bake 15 minutes.

4. *Reduce oven temperature to 350°F.* Continue baking 10 to 15 minutes or until pancake is puffed and golden brown.

5. Serve pancake in skillet with Summer Berries.   *Makes 6 servings*

Summer Berries

2 cups blueberries
1 cup sliced strawberries
1 cup raspberries
Sugar to taste
Whipping cream (optional)

Combine blueberries, strawberries and raspberries in medium bowl. Gently toss with sugar. Let stand 5 minutes. Top with cream, if desired.

Makes 4 cups

Fresh foods

Puff Pancake with Summer Berries   7

Roasted Sweet Pepper Tapas

2 red bell peppers (8 ounces each)
2 tablespoons olive oil
1 clove garlic, minced
1 teaspoon chopped fresh oregano *or* ½ teaspoon dried
    oregano leaves
Garlic bread (optional)
Fresh oregano sprig for garnish

1. Cover broiler pan with foil. Adjust rack so that broiler pan is about 4 inches from heat source. Preheat broiler.

2. Place peppers on foil. Broil 15 to 20 minutes or until blackened on all sides, turning peppers every 5 minutes with tongs.

3. To steam peppers and loosen skin, place blackened peppers in paper bag. Close bag; set aside to cool about 15 to 20 minutes.

4. To peel peppers, cut around core, twist and remove. Cut peppers in half. Peel off skin. Rinse under cold water to remove seeds. Cut pepper halves into ¼-inch-wide strips.

5. Transfer pepper strips to glass jar. Add oil, garlic and oregano. Close lid; shake to blend. Marinate at least 1 hour. Serve with garlic bread, if desired, or refrigerate in jar up to 1 week. Garnish, if desired.

Makes 6 servings

Tip: Use this roasting technique for all types of sweet and hot peppers. Broiling time will vary depending on the size of the pepper. When handling hot peppers (such as Anaheims, jalapeños, poblanos or serranos) wear plastic disposable gloves and use special caution to prevent irritation to skin and eyes. Green bell peppers do not work as well, since their skins are thinner.

Fresh foods

Greens, White Bean and Barley Soup

½ pound carrots, peeled
2 tablespoons olive oil
1½ cups chopped onions
2 cloves garlic, minced
1½ cups sliced mushrooms
6 cups vegetable broth
2 cups cooked barley
1 can (16 ounces) Great Northern beans, rinsed and drained
2 bay leaves
1 teaspoon sugar
1 teaspoon dried thyme leaves
1½ pounds collard greens, washed, stemmed and chopped (about 7 cups)
1 tablespoon white wine vinegar
Hot pepper sauce
Red bell pepper strips for garnish (optional)

1. Cut carrots lengthwise into quarters; cut crosswise into ¼-inch pieces.

2. Heat oil in Dutch oven over medium heat until hot. Add carrots, onions and garlic; cook and stir 3 minutes. Add mushrooms; cook and stir 5 minutes or until tender.

3. Add broth, barley, beans, bay leaves, sugar and thyme. Bring to a boil over high heat. Reduce heat to low. Cover and simmer 5 minutes.

4. Add greens; simmer 10 minutes.

5. Remove bay leaves; discard. Stir in vinegar. Season to taste with pepper sauce. Garnish with red bell pepper strips, if desired.

Makes 8 (1¼-cup) servings

Garden Fresh Gazpacho

4 large tomatoes (about 2 pounds)
1 large cucumber, peeled and seeded
½ red bell pepper, seeded
½ green bell pepper, seeded
½ red onion
3 cloves garlic
¼ cup *Frank's® RedHot®* Cayenne Pepper Sauce
¼ cup red wine vinegar
3 tablespoons olive oil
2 tablespoons minced fresh basil
1 teaspoon salt
Additional 2 cups chopped mixed fresh vegetables, such as tomatoes, bell peppers, cucumbers and green onions

1. Coarsely chop 4 tomatoes, 1 cucumber, ½ red bell pepper, ½ green bell pepper, ½ red onion and garlic; place in food processor or blender. Add *Frank's RedHot* Sauce, vinegar, oil, basil and salt. Cover; process until very smooth. (Process in batches if necessary.) Transfer soup to large glass serving bowl.

2. Stir in additional chopped vegetables, leaving some for garnish, if desired. Cover; refrigerate 1 hour before serving.

Makes 6 servings (6 cups)

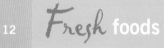

California Crab Salad

1 packet (.4 ounce) HIDDEN VALLEY® The Original Ranch® Buttermilk Recipe Salad Dressing Mix
1 cup buttermilk
1 cup mayonnaise
1 tablespoon grated fresh ginger
1 teaspoon prepared horseradish
2 cups cooked white rice, chilled
4 lettuce leaves
8 ounces cooked crabmeat, chilled
1 large ripe avocado, thinly sliced
½ medium cucumber, thinly sliced

In medium bowl, whisk together salad dressing mix, buttermilk and mayonnaise. Whisk in ginger and horseradish. Cover and refrigerate 30 minutes. To serve, arrange ½ cup rice on top of each lettuce leaf. Top with 2 tablespoons of the dressing. Arrange one quarter of the crabmeat, avocado and cucumber on top of each rice mound. Serve with remaining dressing. Garnish with cherry tomatoes and lime wedges, if desired.

Makes 4 servings

Italian Tortellini Salad

2 cups broccoli florets
½ cup sliced carrot
8 ounces tortellini, cooked and cooled
1 cup (6 ounces) CURE 81® ham cut into strips
1 cup sliced green bell pepper
1 cup sliced red bell pepper
½ cup sliced red onion
½ cup creamy Italian salad dressing

Cook broccoli and carrot in boiling water 2 to 3 minutes or until crisp-tender; drain. Cool. In large bowl, combine broccoli, carrot, cooked tortellini, ham, bell peppers and onion. Toss with dressing. *Makes 4 servings*

Mandarin Turkey Salad with Buttermilk-Herb Dressing

Buttermilk-Herb Dressing (recipe follows)
1 can (about 14 ounces) chicken broth
1¼ pounds turkey tenderloins, cut in half lengthwise
½ teaspoon dried basil leaves
½ pound (about 8 cups) mesclun salad greens, washed and dried
2 pounds (about 10 cups) raw cut-up vegetables, such as broccoli florets, red or yellow bell peppers, carrots and red onion
1 can (11 ounces) mandarin orange segments, drained

1. Prepare Buttermilk-Herb Dressing. Cover and refrigerate.

2. Place broth in medium saucepan; bring to a boil over high heat. Add turkey and basil. Return to a boil; reduce heat. Simmer, covered, 12 to 14 minutes or until turkey is no longer pink.

3. Remove turkey from broth. When cool enough to handle, shred turkey into strips.

4. Arrange salad greens on individual plates. Divide turkey evenly over salad greens. Arrange vegetables and orange segments around turkey; drizzle each serving with 2 tablespoons Buttermilk-Herb Dressing.

Makes 6 servings

Buttermilk-Herb Dressing

½ cup plus 1 tablespoon buttermilk
3 tablespoons raspberry-flavored vinegar
1 tablespoon chopped fresh basil leaves
1½ teaspoons snipped fresh chives
¼ teaspoon minced garlic

Place all ingredients in small bowl; stir to combine.   *Makes about ¾ cup*

 *Fresh* foods

Pepper Stuffed Flank Steak with Chef's Signature Steak Sauce

1 flank steak (about 1½ pounds)
Salt
Ground black pepper
2 cups thinly sliced bell peppers (green, red and/or yellow)
1 small onion, thinly sliced
Chef's Signature Steak Sauce (recipe follows)

Lay steak flat on baking sheet lined with plastic wrap. Cover and freeze about 2 hours or until nearly firm. Place steak on cutting board. Hold large sharp knife parallel to steak. Carefully cut steak in half lengthwise. Thaw in refrigerator until steak can be rolled up easily. Sprinkle inside of each piece of meat with salt and black pepper. Arrange bell peppers and onion on meat, leaving ½-inch edge around meat. Tightly roll up jelly-roll style; tie with kitchen string or secure with toothpicks. (Soak toothpicks in water 20 minutes before using, to prevent burning.)

Prepare Chef's Signature Steak Sauce; set aside. Place steak on oiled grid. Grill over medium-hot coals 25 minutes for medium doneness, turning often. Baste with some of Chef's Signature Steak Sauce during last 10 minutes of grilling. Remove string or toothpicks. Let stand 5 minutes. Slice diagonally. Serve with remaining sauce. *Makes 6 servings*

Chef's Signature Steak Sauce

½ cup ketchup
¼ cup *French's*® Worcestershire Sauce
1 to 2 tablespoons *Frank's*® *RedHot*® Cayenne Pepper Sauce
2 cloves garlic, minced

Combine ingredients in small bowl; stir until smooth. *Makes ¾ cup*

Prep Time: 30 minutes
Freeze Time: 2 hours
Cook Time: 25 minutes

Mushroom Pasta Scampi

    8 ounces uncooked linguine
    2 tablespoons olive oil
    1 pound fresh white mushrooms, sliced
    1 tablespoon chopped garlic
    1 pound frozen peeled and deveined raw large shrimp, thawed*
   10 ounces fresh spinach, trimmed and torn into pieces (about 7 cups)
    ¼ cup grated Parmesan cheese
    ¼ teaspoon crushed red pepper

*To quickly thaw shrimp: Place in a colander with cold running water for about 8 minutes; drain thoroughly.

Cook linguine according to package directions. Drain, reserving ½ cup pasta water; set aside. Meanwhile, heat olive oil in large skillet. Add mushrooms and garlic; cook and stir about 5 minutes or until tender and mushroom liquid is almost evaporated. Add shrimp; cover and cook about 5 minutes or until shrimp is almost cooked through. Stir in spinach and reserved ½ cup pasta water, if desired. Cover and cook about 1 minute or until spinach is wilted. Place pasta in serving bowl; stir in mushroom and shrimp mixture, Parmesan cheese and red pepper. Toss to combine. Season with salt, if desired.   *Makes 4 servings*

Favorite recipe from **Mushroom Council**

Fresh foods

Curried Chicken & Potato Wraps

Mango Salsa (page 23)
6 (8-inch) flour tortillas
Nonstick cooking spray
1 medium onion, chopped
2 tablespoons minced fresh ginger
2 tablespoons minced garlic (10 to 12 cloves)
12 ounces boneless skinless chicken thighs, cut into 1-inch pieces
1 tablespoon curry powder
¼ teaspoon ground red pepper
1 can (about 14 ounces) chicken broth
2 large potatoes (about 1 pound), peeled and cut into ½-inch cubes
½ cup raisins
¼ cup cider vinegar
2 tablespoons brown sugar
¼ cup chopped fresh cilantro

1. Prepare Mango Salsa. Wrap flour tortillas in plastic; set aside.

2. Spray large nonstick skillet with cooking spray; heat over high heat. Add onion, ginger and garlic; cook and stir 4 minutes or until onion is crisp-tender and golden. Add chicken; cook, without stirring, 4 minutes or until golden. Turn chicken; cook 2 minutes more.

3. Add curry powder and red pepper to skillet; cook and stir 30 seconds or until fragrant. Stir in chicken broth, potatoes, raisins, vinegar and brown sugar; bring to a boil. Reduce heat to low; partially cover and simmer 30 minutes or until potatoes are tender when pierced. Uncover; simmer, gently stirring, until most liquid is absorbed. Remove from heat; stir in cilantro.

4. Place tortillas in microwave and microwave at HIGH 1 to 2 minutes or until pliable. Spoon chicken mixture onto center of tortillas. Top with Mango Salsa. Fold all 4 sides of tortillas over filling.   *Makes 6 servings*

Mango Salsa

1 large ripe mango, peeled and cubed
3 tablespoons lime juice
2 tablespoons minced fresh cilantro or fresh mint leaves

Combine all ingredients in small bowl.   *Makes about 1 cup*

Italian Grilled Vegetables

4 medium red potatoes, unpeeled
2 tablespoons orange juice
1 tablespoon balsamic vinegar
1 clove garlic, minced
½ teaspoon salt
¼ teaspoon black pepper
⅓ cup plus 3 tablespoons olive oil, divided
8 thin slices (4×2 inches each) ham or prosciutto
3 ounces garlic-flavored soft goat cheese, cut into 8 pieces
8 asparagus spears
1 *each* red and yellow bell peppers, cut in half and stems and seeds removed
2 small zucchini, cut lengthwise into thin slices
1 Japanese eggplant, cut lengthwise into ¼-inch-thick slices
12 large mushrooms
2 poblano or green bell peppers, cut in half and stems and seeds removed

1. Prepare grill for direct grilling. Cook potatoes in boiling water until tender. Drain; cool slightly. Cut potatoes into thick slices. Meanwhile, combine juice, vinegar, garlic, salt and black pepper in small bowl; whisk in ⅓ cup oil. Set aside.

2. Wrap each ham slice around 1 piece cheese and 1 asparagus spear. Thread cheese bundles onto wooden skewers. (Soak wooden skewers in hot water 30 minutes to prevent burning.) Brush bundles with remaining 3 tablespoons oil.

3. Grill bell peppers, skin side down, over medium heat 8 minutes or until skins are charred. Place in large resealable plastic food storage bag; seal. Let stand 5 minutes; discard skins. Grill remaining vegetables on covered grill over medium heat 2 to 5 minutes on each side or until tender. Grill cheese bundles over medium heat until lightly browned. Arrange vegetables and cheese bundles in large glass dish; drizzle with juice mixture, turning to coat. Let stand 15 minutes. *Makes 8 servings*

Fresh foods

Plum Streusel

Plum Filling
- ½ cup firmly packed light brown sugar
- 3 tablespoons cornstarch
- ½ teaspoon ground nutmeg
- 2½ pounds ripe plums, pitted and sliced ½ inch thick

Streusel
- 1 cup all-purpose flour
- ½ Butter Flavor CRISCO® Stick or ½ cup Butter Flavor CRISCO® all-vegetable shortening
- ½ cup firmly packed light brown sugar
- 1 teaspoon ground cinnamon
- 1 teaspoon vanilla
- ¼ teaspoon salt

1. Heat oven to 350°F. Spray 3-quart shallow baking dish with CRISCO® No-Stick Cooking Spray; set aside.

2. For filling, combine ½ cup brown sugar, cornstarch and nutmeg in large bowl; mix well. Add plums and stir gently to coat evenly. Place in prepared pan.

3. For streusel, combine flour, shortening, ½ cup brown sugar, cinnamon, vanilla and salt in large bowl. Mix with fork until mixture is combined and just crumbly. *Do not overmix.* Sprinkle over fruit mixture.

4. Bake at 350°F for 45 minutes or until streusel top is crisp. Cool about 10 minutes; serve warm with whipped cream or ice cream.

Makes 6 to 8 servings

Tip: Streusel is the German word for "sprinkle," and that is exactly how you're going to add the topping. This easy dessert is perfect for summer holiday entertaining.

Fresh foods

Speedy Pineapple-Lime Sorbet

1 ripe pineapple, peeled and cut into cubes (about 4 cups)
⅓ cup frozen limeade concentrate, thawed
1 to 2 tablespoons fresh lime juice
1 teaspoon grated lime peel

1. Arrange pineapple in single layer on large jelly-roll pan; freeze at least 1 hour or until very firm. Transfer pineapple to resealable plastic freezer food storage bag; freeze up to 1 month.

2. Combine frozen pineapple, limeade, lime juice and lime peel in food processor; process until smooth and fluffy. If mixture doesn't become smooth and fluffy, let stand 30 minutes to soften slightly; then repeat processing. Serve immediately. *Makes 8 servings*

Note: This dessert is best if served immediately; but it may be made ahead, stored in the freezer, then softened several minutes before serving.

Fresh foods

Acknowledgments

*The publisher would like to thank the companies
and organizations listed below for the use of
their recipes and photographs in this publication.*

Crisco is a registered trademark of the J.M. Smucker Company

Egg Beaters®

The Hidden Valley® Food Products Company

Hormel Foods, Carapelli USA, LLC and Melting Pot Foods Inc.

Mushroom Information Center

Reckitt Benckiser Inc.

Unilever Foods North America